KU-619-107

Contents

Off-road

Road racing

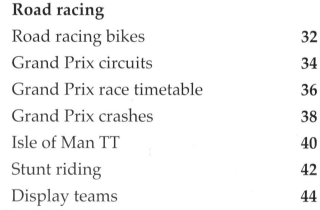

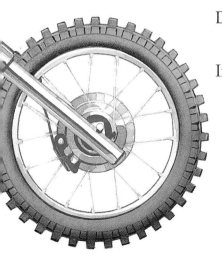

Off-road bikes

Off-road bikes go through a lot of mud. Off-road bikers don't want mud trapped between the tyre and the mudguards, so the bikes have high mudguards. The engine and exhaust pipe are also high off the ground. This is to stop water and mud getting into the engine or the exhaust pipe.

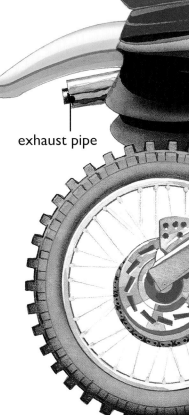

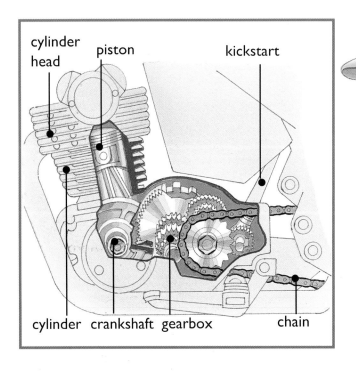

cylinder head

piston

kickstart

exhaust pipe

cylinder   crankshaft   gearbox

chain

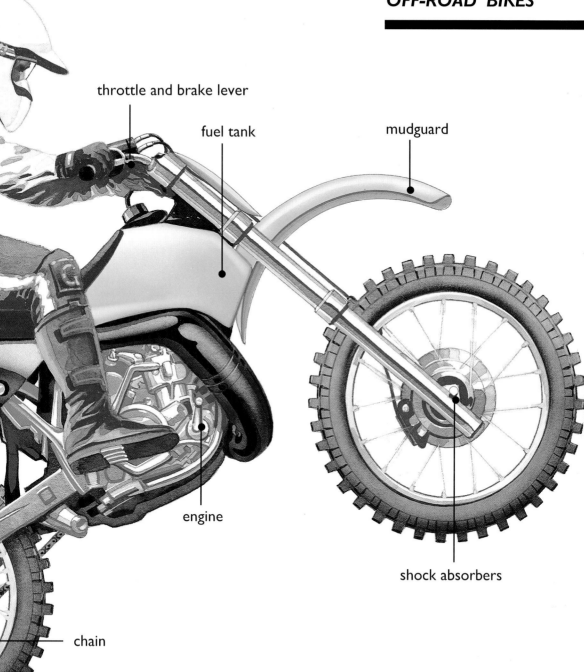

throttle and brake lever

fuel tank

mudguard

engine

shock absorbers

chain

Tyres

Off-road bikes need thick, knobbly tyres to grip in the mud and dirt. The tyres are narrower than on road bikes and they have deeper treads.

There are different tyres for different types of off-road biking.

Enduro

jagged knob pattern
gives good grip

Motorcross

pattern gives good grip
on mud and sand

Shock absorber

The shock absorber consists of a cylinder and a piston inside a thick steel spring. There is oil in the cylinder, and the piston moves up and down in this oil. The piston can't move very fast in the oil. The oil also takes some of the bounce out of the spring. It 'absorbs the shock' and so is called a shock absorber.

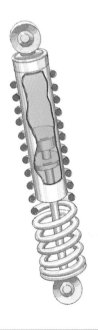

The gear

Helmet
*The helmet is made of glass fibre
or plastic. It is padded inside.
The face guard protects your teeth
and jaw. It must fit properly.*

Body armour

Goggles
*Goggles protect your
eyes from mud and
stones and keep out
the wind and cold.*

Kidney belt

Gloves

Jacket and trousers

Knee and shoulder
protectors

Boots
*Motorcyclist's boots
have metal tips.*

Trials riding

'I started riding in trials events when I was eleven. I joined a club as soon as my dad got me a bike. It was second-hand. We found it in the ads section of a motorbike paper. I wanted a new bike, but Dad said they cost too much. He said he might get me a new bike when I was a better rider.

This is Steve. Here's what he says about trials riding.

I like trials riding because it's tough and exciting. You aren't really racing against other riders. You're riding against the terrain – the terrain is the ground you ride over.

Trials riding is all about skill. You don't go fast. Most of the time you go at a walking pace. It isn't just about speed. You do section work against the clock but there's always enough time. A timed section will be up something like a steep cliff face.

The aim of trials riding is to get round the course without stopping. You mustn't stop, you mustn't put your foot down and you mustn't lose your way. If you stop, you get penalty points. You also get penalty points if you put a foot down, take the wrong course, or fall off. Falling off your bike is a real disaster!

Penalty points

Marshalls stand at special places called 'observed points' and watch you. They know the places where a rider is likely to stop, or is going to put his foot down.

Taking part in a beginners' race

It is difficult to say exactly how many penalty points you get for each thing you do wrong. It depends on which type of race it is. There are a lot of different races, depending on age and experience: Expert, Inter, Novice, Youth, Schoolboy, Beginner, and so on.

The winner might have about 6 penalty points on each lap – you usually do three laps, that's three times round the circuit.

Other riders could have more than 20 penalty points for each lap. The riders who come in last could have 40 or 50 penalty points.

Bikes for trials riding are high off the ground. They have to be because we go up and down steep hills, over rocks, across wet grass. We ride through streams and deep mud. I usually finish covered in mud – that's normal.

The bikes are quiet, they don't roar like the Motorcross bikes which are used for racing. They are tuned differently because they're doing a different job. Like I said, you go really slowly.

We wear much the same gear as other off-road riders, for example, helmet, and boots with steel caps. We don't usually wear body armour, though, just knee and elbow pads. You do get hurt at times, but it's a great sport. Nothing could stop me doing it.'

One of the oldest and most famous trials is the Scottish Six Day Trial. This trial is held around Fort William in Scotland. It was first held in 1909.

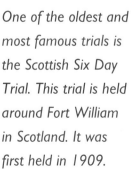

Motocross

COME MOTOCROSS RACING THIS WEEKEND

JOIN IN OR WATCH ONE OF THE MOST EXCITING FORMS OF OFF-ROAD RACING

This is Ian. He started Motocross when he was nine.

'You can start Motocross when you're little – there are kids at my club who are four and five years old. I started when I was nine. Most of the top riders started when they were about seven or eight.

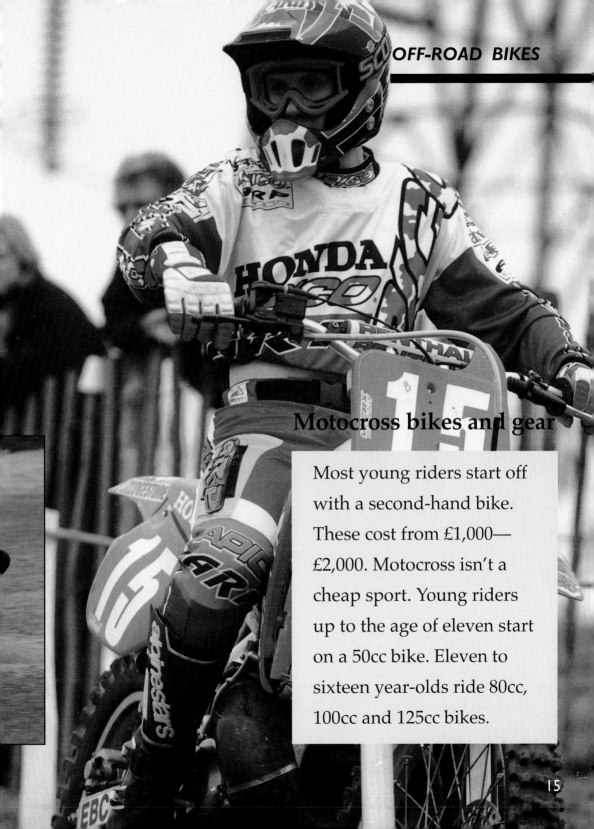

Motocross bikes and gear

Most young riders start off with a second-hand bike. These cost from £1,000—£2,000. Motocross isn't a cheap sport. Young riders up to the age of eleven start on a 50cc bike. Eleven to sixteen year-olds ride 80cc, 100cc and 125cc bikes.

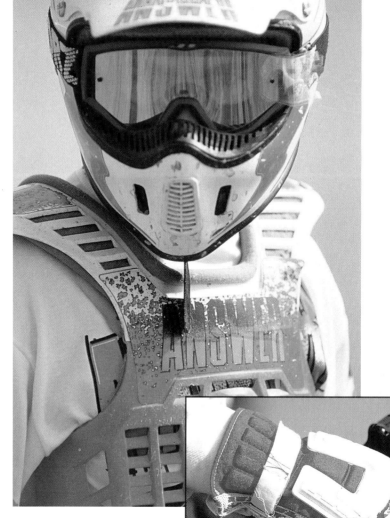

You need a helmet, and you have to get a new one. No one should ever buy a second-hand helmet, because you don't know where it has been, or what has happened to it. You need boots with steel toe caps.

Most Motocross riders wear Motocross jeans. They're made of tough, flexible material and are waterproof.

Clubs

The first thing you have to do when you start Motocross is join a club. The clubs organize the events you ride in and they tell you where the tracks are. These are the tracks where it is OK for you to practise. You can't practise anywhere. Farmers go mad if you start racing round their fields on your bike.

In a club, you start as a cadet. Then you work your way up through the juniors and seniors to the top class – the experts. You race in your group, so you usually race against people of your own age.

Races

Motocross is a race. About 40 of you start together and go round the circuit several times. An event usually lasts for 35—45 minutes. The winner is the one who crosses the line first. It isn't like trials events.

There is no timing, no records to break. Normally, about 30 riders finish a race and the first six are placed.

Motocross is a very tough sport. You have to be fit because you need strong muscles, stamina and quick reactions. You have to train a lot. I train after school and all through the holidays. Then I ride in competitions every weekend. It's hard work, and you can get very muddy. I love it!'

Enduro

This is Helen. She has answered these questions about Enduro.

What is an Enduro?

'Enduros are long distance motorbike races - like the RAC Car Rally. They are usually held over rough country.

What kind of bike do Enduro riders use?

Enduro bikes are off-road machines, much the same as in Motocross – but they're quieter and they have lights because you ride at night in some events. The bikes have to be registered, because you sometimes ride on the road to get from one section to another.

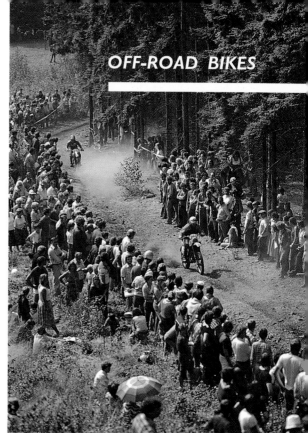

How long is an Enduro circuit?

Enduro circuits can be anything from two miles to over 1,000 miles long. 'Hare and Hounds' events are popular. These have laps of 8 to 12 miles and you see how many laps you can do in three hours. That's good fun.

Does time matter on Enduros?

Yes and no. There are timed sections on full Enduros, so then you're racing against the clock. In other sections there is a time limit and you get penalty points if you don't finish within the time, but the riders are given plenty of time. It isn't hard to stay within the limits.

Is it an international sport?

Oh, yes. The big international events are the events to aim for. On some of those events, riders cycle up to 900 miles in one day, round and round the circuit. Then there are events like the International Six Day Enduro. This was first held in England, near Carlisle. Now it takes place in a different country each year.

Is the International Six Day Enduro the longest?

No. The longest Enduro is the Paris to Dakar. It starts on Christmas Day, and goes on into January – it lasts for 20 days and riders cross the Sahara Desert. They cover more than 1,300 miles.

How do you manage on a long-distance Enduro? Where do you stay?

I take my own tent on my bike. The top Enduro riders are in the factory teams. This means they race for a firm who makes bikes.

Factory team riders have camps set up for them. Mechanics travel ahead of the riders, and there are pit-stops at the end of sections.'

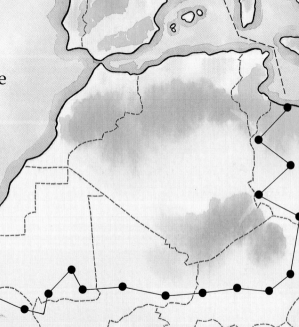

Dakar

Trailbiking

Trailbiking isn't a competitive sport like Motocross and Enduro. You do not ride around a course for points like in trials riding. Trailbiking is a leisure activity. You ride an off-road bike along 'green lanes'. These are off-road tracks in the country.

Advice from LARA - Land Access and Recreation Association

Are you trespassing?

All land in Britain belongs to someone. You don't believe it? Well, it's true. Even wild forests and empty countryside belongs someone. Just because you ha seen other people riding there DOES NOT make it right for yo do the same. They probably ha permission. You need permiss too.

Are you spoiling things for motorsport?

Clubs organize a lot of events for their members and for spectators. They get permission for their riders to use land. They usually pay a lot of money for the permission.

A club may arrange events in a forest on a Sunday. That DOES NOT give you permission to ride in that forest at other times. You must get permission before you ride on ANY land.

NEVER practise for a competition on public paths. Ask your club where you can train.

25

Do you care about the environment?

What looks like a useless tip to you may be home to rare plants, birds and animals. Don't damage important nature sites by careless riding.

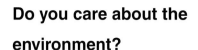

Are you user-friendly?

Think about how you look to other people. Your bike is noisy. It has big, knobbly tyres. Your face is hidden behind a helmet and face mask. You are wearing big boots. No wonder you alarm walkers and locals when you meet them. Don't make enemies for yourself and your sport. Smile, and say hello.

Why not join a club ...?

... and enjoy your sport even more. Even if you don't like clubs and meetings, clubs are helpful. You can learn a lot about your sport, and help the clubs to protect the environment.

Do you care about the law?

It is a criminal offence to drive or ride your bike:

- on the beach, or on sand dunes
- on open moorland
- on commons
- in parks
- over farmland.

Speedway

This is Andrew. He has been riding in speedway races since he was seven.

'I had my first bike when I was three; my dad was a speedway rider, and he wanted me to be a champion. He nearly gave up after I'd been riding for three years without winning. Then I started to win, and as I got older and moved into the senior events, I went on winning.

I enjoy speedway but it's also my job. It's a hard way to earn a living, but I think it beats slaving away in some factory or office. Most of the lads think of it as a job, and they take it seriously. They haven't got many years at the top, so they've got to make the most of them.

There are four riders in a race. They ride 18 heats, each heat is four laps of the circuit.

The bikes don't have any brakes, and it is easy to crash. Most riders get hurt sooner or later.

You don't think about getting hurt when you're waiting to go. You just build up the aggression, you want to get to the corner first, get out in front. You need to get out in front and give everybody else the rubbish off your back wheel. At the same time, you race as a team. You've got to trust the other people on the track, same as they trust you. You're racing against them but off the track you're mates. You're all in it together.'

Speedway riders aren't paid a wage. If they win, they earn money. If they lose, they don't. It's as simple as that.

Speedway is dangerous, as riders ride round a dirt track at 50-60 miles per hour, inches away from each other.

Grass track and ice racing

Grass track

This is soft speedway - but it is still fast and exciting. Again, it's four laps, but this time on smooth, flat grass. The track is oval. Riders compete on solo and sidecar bikes. The machines they ride are specially built for grass track racing. Grass track racing is a good sport for newcomers to motorcycling.

Ice racing

This is a popular sport in
Scandinavia and Eastern
Europe. Riders race against
each other on a solid ice track.
The bikes have special tyres to
grip the ice. These tyres have
strong steel spikes.

Road racing

Road racing bikes

The road-racing bike is a different machine from the off-road bike. For road racing, the bikes are streamlined and have different tyres. The tyres are wider than off-road bikes and riders have smooth tyres for normal use and ones with treads for wet weather.

Some bikes are 500cc. They are very powerful. They are made for racing.

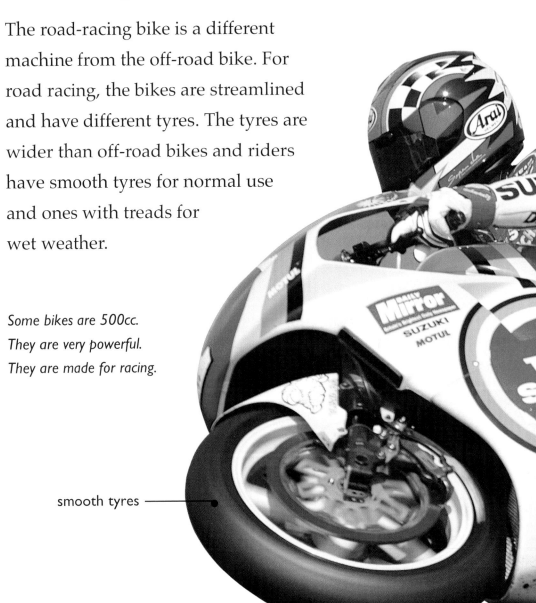

smooth tyres ——

top riders are in a
company team, like
the Suzuki team

casing makes
the bike more
streamlined

Some road races, for example, the Isle of Man race, are held on ordinary roads.

Other road races are held on special race tracks. The Grand Prix Championship races are an example of this.

Grand Prix circuits

Grand Prix motorcycling is like Grand Prix motor-racing. Races are held on circuits around the world.

The Dutch Grand Prix is held at Assen in Holland. The track used to be a public road, but it is now closed off.

It is only used for racing. The track still has a camber - that's where the road is higher in the middle.

The camber is dangerous for riders, especially on 500cc bikes. They find that their rear wheels spin when they turn corners. Most riders prefer racing on a flat track.

Road camber

The Dutch Grand Prix is one of the biggest events of the Grand Prix season. More than 120,000 people from all over Europe go to watch the races.

Grand Prix race timetable

Friday morning
Race practice.

Friday afternoon
Race for grid places. The riders are timed and the best times get the best places on the grid.

Friday night
The team of mechanics make final changes to the bikes. They may work through the night.

Saturday morning
Race practice.

Saturday afternoon
Race for grid places.

Sunday
The Grand Prix race.
Over 20 riders race. They line up in their grid places, and wait for the green light.
Then they're off ....

Points

The riders get points for
where they finish in the race.
These points are added up
and the rider with most points
at the end of the season
becomes world champion.

Grand Prix crashes

The powerful 500cc bikes are difficult to control and riders often crash at speeds of 150 mph.

Here is what happened to one rider at
Assen during the timed practice race.

Schwantz (an American rider) was thrown from his Suzuki going round the Mandeveen corner. He got his left hand trapped under the bouncing bike. Three of his bones were dislocated and a fourth was fractured. By Sunday his hand was very bruised.

Schwantz went on to finish the race! His team made changes to the left handlebar to help him steer. Schwantz led the race for a while, and finally came 5th.

Isle of Man TT

Who won the first TT race, and when?

Charlie Collier won the single-cylinder race. Rem Fowler took first prize in the twin-cylinder class. This was in 1907.

What does TT stand for?

TT stands for Tourist Trophy.

Why did they have races on the Isle of Man?

The British Government wouldn't allow roads to close for TT races. But the Parliament on the Isle of Man allowed some roads to be closed for racing.

Are races still held on the Isle of Man?

Yes. Every year in late May or early June, thousands of fans go to the Isle of Man for TT week. There are many different types of races – for all kinds of bikes.

Are the TT races part of the Grand Prix World Championship?

No. The Isle of Man TT races used to be an important round in the Championship, but in 1976 a lot of the world's top riders wouldn't take part in the races because the circuit was dangerous. The races then stopped being part of the World Championship.

Stunt riding

It takes a lot of nerve to be a stunt rider, and you have to be a very good motorcyclist to do any stunts.

Some stunt riders do stunts by themselves. These are the riders who jump over rows of cars or across a gorge. They ride their motorcycles along a tightrope. Stunt riders ride through flames and ride over all kinds of obstacles.

Stuntmen do film and television work. They may play a policeman or a wild teenager or a despatch rider. Stuntmen are very skilled, very brave and very careful!

There are also team stunt riders, who put on displays. They work as a team, and they know that they rely on the skills of the other team members.

Display teams

Display teams

Display teams perform stunts at tournaments, shows and sporting events. Some display teams are army teams. The Honda Imps are young riders.

Pyramid

This is a 'balance'. There are several riders at the bottom on bikes. They support other riders. One rider is at the top of the pyramid.

Harness

Straps and belts help the riders to perform a balance. They can be attached to the riders, or to the bike and its supports.

Ramp jumping

This is jumping over obstacles from a ramp. The motorcyclist takes off and lands on a ramp.

Wheelie

Riding with the front wheel of the bike lifted up in the air.

Fire jump

A stunt where the rider rides through flames. This is the hoop of fire. The rider rides up a ramp and jumps through a hoop of flames.

Evel Knievel and Eddie Kidd

Two of the most famous stuntsmen ever. Evel Knievel's last stunt was to jump over 13 London buses. But he hurt his back, and did no more stunts. Eddie Kidd jumped over 22 cars.

Index